MASTERING SIX SIGMA:

NAVIGATING DMAIC AND DMADV FOR BUSINESS SUCCESS

T.D ERROL

Mastering Six Sigma:

Navigating DMAIC and DMADV for Business Success

T.D Errol

Mastering Six Sigma: Navigating DMAIC and DMADV For Business Success
by T.D. Errol

Copyright © 2024 by T.D. Errol
All rights reserved. No part of this book may be reproduced or transmitted in any form or by any means, electronic or mechanical, including photocopying, recording, or by any information storage and retrieval system, without the prior written permission of the publisher, except where permitted by law.

Published by Errol Publishing

This is a work of nonfiction. Names, characters, businesses, places, events, and incidents are either the products of the author's imagination or used in a fictitious manner. Any resemblance to actual persons, living or dead, or actual events is purely coincidental.

Cover Design by Clifford Daiss
Edited by Clifford Daiss

First Edition: August, 2024

ISBN: 9798336034684
Imprint: Independently published

Printed in the United States of America

Disclaimer

The information in this book is provided with the understanding that the author and publisher are not rendering professional advice or services to the individual reader. The contents of this book are for informational purposes only and should not be used as a substitute for professional advice.

Author Bio

T.D. Errol is an author and adventurer residing in the picturesque state of Colorado. With a deep appreciation for the beauty and tranquility of the outdoors, T.D. finds solace and inspiration in nature's embrace. Though the days of conquering the rugged Rocky Mountains may be in the past, T.D. continues to revel in the simple pleasure of walking, using it as a means of exploration and introspection.

Having served as a United States Marine Corps infantryman, T.D. possesses a unique perspective on the therapeutic power of walking. Battling through various injuries, including a recent back surgery that fused three vertebrae, T.D. intimately understands the challenges and triumphs of the recovery process. It is through this personal journey that T.D. has developed a revolutionary theory on walking, one that emphasizes the significance of each step taken rather than the speed or distance covered. By embracing the simplicity and mindfulness of intentional walking, T.D. has discovered a renewed sense of health and well-being.

Driven by a genuine passion to share these profound insights and experiences, T.D. aspires to inspire others to unlock the transformative potential of walking. Through captivating storytelling and practical guidance, T.D. imparts wisdom gained from a lifetime of self-development, management skills, and an unwavering dedication to personal growth. Drawing upon years of leadership and managerial roles, T.D. remains committed to staying abreast of the latest trends in these fields, offering a wealth of knowledge to the next generation of leaders.

With a captivating writing style and a genuine desire to uplift and empower, T.D. Errol invites readers to embark on a transformative journey of self-discovery, harnessing the healing powers of walking and embracing the limitless potential of personal growth.

Other Books by T.D. Errol

Kanban Life: Visualize Your Productivity

The Power of Checklists: Mastering momentum for Business Success

Decisive Choices: Mastering Strategies for Effective Decision Making and Problem Solving

Digitize Your Life: Embrace Sustainability and Efficiency

Embracing Change and Adapting: The Importance of being open to change and how to adapt to new situations or environments as part of personal growth.

The Evolving Self: Mastering Continuous Improvement in the Prime of Life

Mastering Knowledge in the Digital Age: A Young Professional's Guide to PKM

Think Smart: Mastering Problem Solving and Critical Thinking for Professional Success

Tiny Triumphs: The Power of Micro Steps in Achieving Continuous Improvement

Share Your Thoughts with Us!

Dear Reader,

I hope you enjoyed journeying through the pages of my book. Your insights and experiences mean the world to me. If the story resonated with you or if there's any area you feel could be improved, I'd be truly grateful to hear your thoughts.

Please consider leaving a review on Amazon or the platform where you made the purchase. Your feedback not only helps me grow as an author but also guides fellow readers in their choices.

Alternatively, feel free to drop me a personal note at Errol_publishing@aol.com. Every word you share contributes to the story's evolving journey.

Thank you for being a cherished part of this adventure.

Warm regards,

T.D. Errol

Dedication

To Anne,
my north star, the fabric that wraps and warms my heart and soul. Your unwavering support and endless love make every journey worthwhile.

And to Ema,
my faithful companion, who walks by my side with unyielding loyalty. Your presence fills my days with joy and your spirit with unconditional love.

Forward

In today's competitive business environment, the difference between success and failure often hinges on a company's ability to innovate, streamline processes, and consistently deliver high-quality products and services. Six Sigma has long been recognized as a powerful methodology for achieving these goals, offering a systematic approach to process improvement that is both rigorous and adaptable.

"Mastering Six Sigma: Navigating DMAIC and DMADV for Business Success" is not just another book on quality management; it is a comprehensive guide designed to take you deep into the heart of two of Six Sigma's most essential methodologies: DMAIC and DMADV. Whether your goal is to optimize existing processes or to create new ones that exceed customer expectations, this book provides the tools, insights, and strategies needed to succeed.

The journey through DMAIC and DMADV is one of discovery and refinement. DMAIC, with its focus on improving current processes, offers a structured path for identifying inefficiencies, reducing variation, and achieving better outcomes. DMADV, on the other hand, is your blueprint for designing new processes that are robust and customer-focused, ensuring quality from the very beginning.

What sets this book apart is its commitment to blending theory with practical application. Here, you will find detailed explanations of each phase of DMAIC and DMADV, enriched with case studies and examples from various industries. These real-world applications illustrate how the principles of Six Sigma can be adapted to meet the unique challenges of any business.

As you delve into this book, you will discover that Six Sigma is more than just a set of tools—it is a philosophy that encourages continuous improvement, data-driven decision-making, and a relentless focus on customer satisfaction. Mastery of these methodologies can lead to transformative results, both in terms of process efficiency and overall business performance.

It is with great enthusiasm that I introduce this book to you. Whether you are new to Six Sigma or a seasoned practitioner, you will find valuable insights within these pages that will enhance your understanding and application of these powerful methodologies. I hope that *"Mastering Six Sigma: Navigating DMAIC and DMADV for Business Success"* will serve as both an inspiration and a practical guide as you embark on or continue your journey toward operational excellence.

Table of Contents

Introduction	12
Chapter 1: Foundations of Six Sigma	19
Chapter 2: Understanding DMAIC	26
Chapter 3: Understanding DMADV	37
Chapter 4: Tools and Techniques for DMAIC	46
Chapter 5: Tools and Techniques for DMADV	55
Chapter 6: Integrating DMAIC and DMADV in Business Strategy	64
Chapter 7: Overcoming Challenges in Implementation	72
Chapter 8: Measuring and Sustaining Success	78
Chapter 9: The Future of Six Sigma	85
Conclusion	90
Appendices	94

Introduction

Understanding Six Sigma:

Overview of Six Sigma Principles and Its Importance in Process Improvement

Six Sigma is a disciplined, data-driven approach and methodology for eliminating defects in any process. Developed by Motorola in the 1980s and popularized by General Electric, Six Sigma has become a global standard for quality improvement. The methodology aims to improve the quality of process outputs by identifying and removing the causes of defects and minimizing variability in manufacturing and business processes. Six Sigma's core objective is to reach a level of performance where only 3.4 defects occur per million opportunities, which translates to nearly flawless performance.

At the heart of Six Sigma are five key principles: **Define, Measure, Analyze, Improve, and Control (DMAIC)**. These principles guide practitioners in systematically improving processes by focusing on understanding the problem, gathering relevant data, analyzing the root cause of issues, implementing solutions, and establishing controls to sustain improvements. The DMAIC framework is particularly effective in existing process optimization, providing a structured approach to problem-solving that has been adopted by organizations worldwide.

Another critical aspect of Six Sigma is the **Define, Measure, Analyze, Design, and Verify (DMADV)** methodology, used primarily for designing new processes or products at Six Sigma quality levels. While

DMAIC focuses on improving existing processes, DMADV is geared towards process design or re-design to achieve better quality standards from the outset.

The importance of Six Sigma in process improvement cannot be overstated. It offers numerous benefits, including increased efficiency, reduced costs, improved customer satisfaction, and enhanced profitability. By employing a rigorous and quantitative approach to quality management, Six Sigma enables organizations to achieve consistent, high-quality results that meet or exceed customer expectations.

Moreover, Six Sigma fosters a culture of continuous improvement and data-driven decision-making within organizations. It empowers employees at all levels to contribute to process optimization and quality enhancement, driving innovation and competitive advantage. As businesses face increasing pressure to deliver superior products and services, Six Sigma's principles provide a robust framework for achieving operational excellence and maintaining a sustainable edge in the marketplace.

Through this book, you will explore the foundational elements of Six Sigma, delve into the DMAIC and DMADV methodologies, and learn how to apply these principles effectively in your business environment. Whether you are a seasoned practitioner or new to Six Sigma, this comprehensive guide will equip you with the knowledge and tools to navigate Six Sigma for business success.

The Role of DMAIC and DMADV:

Introduction to DMAIC and DMADV as Core Methodologies within Six Sigma

At the heart of Six Sigma are two core methodologies: DMAIC and DMADV. These methodologies provide structured approaches to process improvement and innovation, each designed to address specific needs within an organization. While they share a foundation in statistical analysis and a commitment to quality, their applications and objectives differ significantly.

DMAIC, which stands for Define, Measure, Analyze, Improve, and Control, is a methodology used to improve existing processes. It provides a roadmap for identifying problems, analyzing root causes, and implementing sustainable solutions. Each phase of DMAIC serves a distinct purpose:

- ➤ **Define**: The Define phase is about setting the scope and goals of the project. It involves identifying the problem, defining customer requirements, and establishing clear objectives. This phase is crucial for aligning the project with business goals and ensuring that all stakeholders have a shared understanding of the project's aims.

- ➤ **Measure**: In the Measure phase, data is collected to establish a baseline for current performance. This phase involves identifying key metrics, developing data collection plans, and ensuring the accuracy and reliability of the data. By understanding the current state, organizations can identify areas of variation and waste that need addressing.

- ➤ **Analyze**: The Analyze phase focuses on identifying the root causes of defects or inefficiencies. Through data analysis and process mapping, organizations can pinpoint factors contributing to the problem. This phase is critical for developing effective solutions based on evidence rather than assumptions.

- ➤ **Improve**: During the Improve phase, solutions are developed and implemented to address the root causes identified in the Analyze phase. This may involve process redesign, technology implementation, or changes in workflow. The focus is on creating measurable improvements that align with the project's goals.

- **Control**: The final phase, Control, involves implementing controls to sustain the improvements achieved. This phase ensures that changes are embedded in the organization's processes, preventing regression to previous performance levels. It includes monitoring systems, documentation, and training to maintain the gains made.

DMADV, on the other hand, stands for Define, Measure, Analyze, Design, and Verify, and is used primarily for designing new processes or products. It is particularly valuable when existing processes are inadequate for achieving desired quality levels or when developing innovative products. Each phase of DMADV is focused on creating robust designs that meet customer requirements:

- **Define**: Similar to DMAIC, the Define phase in DMADV sets the project's scope and objectives, emphasizing customer needs and market demands.
- **Measure**: In DMADV, the Measure phase involves identifying and understanding customer needs and translating them into specific requirements for the new process or product.
- **Analyze**: The Analyze phase in DMADV is about exploring various design options and evaluating them against customer requirements. It involves risk assessment and feasibility studies to ensure that the design meets quality standards.
- **Design**: The Design phase involves developing detailed designs and specifications for the process or product. This phase focuses on optimizing the design to meet customer needs while minimizing cost and complexity.
- **Verify**: In the Verify phase, the design is tested and validated to ensure it meets all requirements and performs as expected. This may involve prototype testing, pilot runs, and customer feedback.

Together, DMAIC and DMADV form the backbone of Six Sigma's approach to quality management. By offering structured methodologies tailored to different objectives, they enable organizations to improve existing processes and innovate new ones, driving continuous improvement and excellence. Throughout this book, you will gain a deeper understanding of these methodologies and learn how to apply them effectively to achieve your business goals.

Objectives of the Book:

What Readers Will Gain from Understanding and Applying These Methodologies

The journey through "Mastering Six Sigma: Navigating DMAIC and DMADV for Business Success" is designed to equip readers with the knowledge, skills, and confidence to implement Six Sigma methodologies effectively. This book aims to serve as a comprehensive guide, offering valuable insights into the intricacies of Six Sigma, from foundational principles to advanced applications.

Readers can expect to gain a thorough understanding of both the DMAIC and DMADV methodologies, discovering how these approaches can be tailored to various organizational contexts. Whether you are an executive aiming to drive strategic improvements, a manager seeking to enhance team performance, or a professional eager to refine your skills, this book will provide you with the tools and insights needed to excel.

One of the primary objectives of this book is to demystify the complexities of Six Sigma, making it accessible and actionable for readers at all levels of experience. By breaking down each phase of DMAIC and DMADV into clear, manageable steps, the book ensures that readers can confidently navigate the process improvement landscape. Through practical examples, case studies, and real-world scenarios, you will see how these methodologies have been successfully applied across various industries, demonstrating their versatility and effectiveness.

In addition to methodological understanding, this book emphasizes the strategic integration of Six Sigma into business operations. You will learn how to align Six Sigma projects with organizational goals, ensuring that efforts yield tangible benefits and drive competitive advantage. The book also addresses the importance of fostering a culture of continuous improvement, empowering employees to contribute to quality enhancement and innovation.

As you progress through the book, you will gain valuable insights into the tools and techniques that underpin Six Sigma's success. From data analysis and process mapping to design thinking and risk assessment, you will become proficient in the skills necessary to lead impactful projects and achieve exceptional results.

Ultimately, this book aims to inspire readers to embrace the Six Sigma mindset, fostering a commitment to excellence and a passion for improvement. By understanding and applying these methodologies, you will be equipped to tackle complex challenges, seize opportunities for growth, and elevate the standards of quality within your organization. Whether you are embarking on your first Six Sigma project or seeking to refine your expertise, this book will serve as a trusted companion on your journey toward mastering Six Sigma for business success.

Chapter 1: Foundations of Six Sigma

History and Evolution:

Origins of Six Sigma and Its Development Over Time

The origins of Six Sigma can be traced back to the early 1980s when it was first conceptualized at Motorola. The company faced significant challenges with product quality and customer satisfaction, which spurred a radical transformation in how they approached quality control. Bill Smith, a Motorola engineer, is often credited with developing the Six Sigma methodology. Smith recognized that defects and errors were primarily caused by variations in the manufacturing process and sought to create a systematic approach to minimize these variations.

The term "Six Sigma" itself refers to a statistical concept that measures a process's capability to produce defect-free work. In statistical terms, achieving Six Sigma means operating at a level where the likelihood of producing a defect is extremely low, approximately 3.4 defects per million opportunities. This ambitious target set a new benchmark for quality and excellence, transforming how companies worldwide approached process improvement.

Motorola's adoption of Six Sigma was transformative. By rigorously applying its principles, the company achieved substantial improvements in product quality, reduced costs, and increased customer satisfaction. Motorola's success with Six Sigma did not go unnoticed, and soon other organizations began to take note.

One of the most notable champions of Six Sigma was General Electric (GE) under the leadership of CEO Jack Welch in the mid-1990s. Welch recognized Six Sigma's potential to drive significant improvements across GE's diverse business units. By investing heavily in Six Sigma training and implementation, GE realized billions of dollars in cost savings and productivity gains. The success of Six Sigma at GE played a crucial role in popularizing the methodology globally, establishing it as a key driver of quality and efficiency in both manufacturing and service sectors.

Over the years, Six Sigma has continued to evolve, adapting to the changing needs of businesses and incorporating new tools and techniques. It has expanded beyond its manufacturing roots to encompass a wide range of industries, including healthcare, finance, information technology, and more. The integration of Lean principles, which focus on waste reduction and process efficiency, has further enhanced Six Sigma's applicability and effectiveness.

Today, Six Sigma is recognized as a vital component of modern quality management systems, offering a structured framework for achieving operational excellence. Its evolution reflects the dynamic nature of business environments and the ongoing pursuit of higher quality standards and customer satisfaction. As organizations face increasing competitive pressures and customer expectations, Six Sigma remains a powerful tool for driving innovation and maintaining a sustainable edge in the marketplace.

Throughout this book, you will explore the foundational elements of Six Sigma, including its historical context and evolution, to gain a deeper understanding of how this methodology has shaped the landscape of quality management and continues to drive success in today's business world.

Key Concepts and Terminology:

Definitions of Critical Terms and Concepts

To fully grasp the power and potential of Six Sigma, it is essential to understand its key concepts and terminology. These foundational elements provide the language and framework for Six Sigma methodologies, guiding practitioners in their quest for quality improvement and process excellence.

At the core of Six Sigma is the concept of **variation**. Variation refers to the inevitable differences that occur in any process, resulting in inconsistencies in output quality. Six Sigma seeks to minimize variation through data-driven analysis and process optimization, ensuring that products and services meet customer specifications consistently.

Defects are any instance where a product or service fails to meet customer expectations or specifications. The goal of Six Sigma is to reduce the number of defects to a minimum, ideally achieving a defect rate of 3.4 per million opportunities, which represents a Six Sigma level of quality.

Process capability is a measure of a process's ability to produce output within specified limits. It is a critical metric in Six Sigma, used to assess whether a process is capable of meeting customer requirements consistently. A process with high capability is less likely to produce defects and more likely to deliver high-quality results.

DMAIC is an acronym for Define, Measure, Analyze, Improve, and Control, a structured methodology used to improve existing processes. Each phase of DMAIC plays a vital role in identifying and addressing the root causes of process inefficiencies and defects, leading to sustainable improvements.

DMADV, which stands for Define, Measure, Analyze, Design, and Verify, is a methodology used for designing new processes or products.

It emphasizes the importance of understanding customer requirements and designing solutions that meet or exceed those needs.

Critical to Quality (CTQ) are the key measurable characteristics of a product or process that are essential to meet customer expectations. Identifying CTQ's is crucial in Six Sigma projects, as they help prioritize efforts and focus resources on the most impactful areas.

Sigma level is a statistical measure of process performance, indicating how often defects are likely to occur. A higher sigma level signifies fewer defects and higher quality. Achieving Six Sigma, or a sigma level of six, means that a process operates with near perfection, producing only 3.4 defects per million opportunities.

Lean Six Sigma is an integrated approach that combines the principles of Lean, which focuses on waste reduction and efficiency, with Six Sigma's emphasis on quality improvement and defect reduction. Lean Six Sigma aims to enhance process efficiency while maintaining high-quality standards.

Process mapping is a visual representation of a process, outlining each step and its relationship to other steps. It is a valuable tool in Six Sigma for understanding process flow, identifying bottlenecks, and uncovering opportunities for improvement.

Root cause analysis is a problem-solving method used to identify the underlying causes of defects or issues. By addressing root causes rather than symptoms, Six Sigma practitioners can implement more effective and lasting solutions.

Understanding these key concepts and terminology is fundamental to mastering Six Sigma methodologies. Throughout this book, you will see how these concepts are applied in various contexts, providing a solid foundation for implementing Six Sigma successfully in your organization.

The Importance of Quality Management:

How Six Sigma Fits into Broader Quality Management Practices

In today's competitive business environment, quality management is a critical component of organizational success. It encompasses a wide range of practices and methodologies aimed at ensuring products and services meet or exceed customer expectations. Six Sigma plays a vital role within this broader framework, offering a structured and data-driven approach to achieving and maintaining high-quality standards.

Quality management is centered around the idea that organizations must continuously improve their processes to deliver superior value to customers. This involves understanding customer needs, setting quality objectives, and implementing systems to monitor and improve performance. Six Sigma contributes to these goals by providing a systematic methodology for identifying and eliminating defects, reducing variability, and optimizing processes.

One of the key ways Six Sigma fits into quality management is through its focus on customer satisfaction. By identifying Critical to Quality (CTQ) characteristics and aligning processes with customer requirements, Six Sigma ensures that organizations deliver products and services that meet the highest standards. This customer-centric approach is a cornerstone of quality management, emphasizing the importance of meeting and exceeding customer expectations.

Six Sigma also complements other quality management frameworks, such as Total Quality Management (TQM) and ISO 9001. While TQM focuses on fostering a culture of continuous improvement across the organization, Six Sigma provides the tools and techniques to achieve specific quality improvements. ISO 9001, a widely recognized quality management standard, shares many principles with Six Sigma, including a focus on process improvement and customer satisfaction.

In addition to its alignment with other quality management practices, Six Sigma offers unique advantages that enhance its effectiveness. Its reliance on statistical analysis and data-driven decision-making ensures that improvements are based on empirical evidence rather than intuition. This rigorous approach minimizes the risk of implementing ineffective solutions and enhances the likelihood of achieving sustainable results.

Moreover, Six Sigma's structured methodologies, DMAIC and DMADV, provide clear and repeatable processes for tackling quality issues. This consistency is crucial in quality management, where organizations must be able to replicate successes and build on past achievements. By standardizing the approach to process improvement, Six Sigma helps organizations achieve greater predictability and reliability in their operations.

The importance of quality management extends beyond operational efficiency; it is a key driver of business success. High-quality products and services enhance brand reputation, increase customer loyalty, and lead to greater market share and profitability. By integrating Six Sigma into their quality management practices, organizations can unlock these benefits and position themselves as leaders in their industries.

As you progress through this book, you will discover how Six Sigma fits within the broader landscape of quality management, learning how to leverage its methodologies to drive continuous improvement and achieve excellence in your organization. Through practical insights and real-world examples, you will gain the knowledge and skills needed to harness the full potential of Six Sigma in your pursuit of quality.

Chapter 2:
Understanding DMAIC

Overview of DMAIC:

The Five Phases—Define, Measure, Analyze, Improve, Control

DMAIC, an acronym for Define, Measure, Analyze, and Control, is a structured methodology central to Six Sigma, designed to improve existing processes systematically. Each phase of DMAIC serves a distinct purpose, guiding practitioners through a logical sequence of steps that lead to significant improvements in process performance and quality.

Define

The Define phase is the foundation of the DMAIC process, where the project's scope, objectives, and goals are established. This phase involves identifying the problem to be addressed, defining customer requirements, and setting clear, measurable objectives that align with business goals. Key activities in this phase include:

- **Project Charter**: Developing a project charter that outlines the problem statement, project objectives, scope, timeline, and key stakeholders. The charter serves as a guiding document that ensures all team members are aligned with the project's goals.

- **Voice of the Customer (VoC)**: Collecting and analyzing customer feedback to understand their needs and expectations. This step helps identify Critical to Quality (CTQ) characteristics, which are essential for meeting customer requirements.

- **High-Level Process Mapping**: Creating a high-level map of the process to visualize its flow and identify key inputs and outputs. This map provides a baseline understanding of the process and helps pinpoint areas for improvement.

Measure

In the Measure phase, data is collected to establish a baseline of the current process performance. This phase focuses on quantifying the problem and identifying the process's key metrics. Key activities in this phase include:

- **Data Collection Plan**: Developing a plan for collecting data that ensures accuracy, reliability, and relevance. This plan outlines the data sources, collection methods, and tools used for measurement.
- **Process Capability Analysis**: Evaluating the process's ability to meet customer requirements consistently. This analysis helps identify areas of variation and assess the process's performance relative to specifications.
- **Measurement System Analysis (MSA)**: Assessing the accuracy and precision of the measurement system to ensure that data collected is reliable and valid.

Analyze

The Analyze phase involves identifying the root causes of defects or inefficiencies within the process. This phase uses data analysis and statistical tools to uncover underlying issues that contribute to process variation. Key activities in this phase include:

- **Root Cause Analysis**: Using techniques such as the Fishbone Diagram and 5 Whys to identify the root causes of problems. This step focuses on understanding the factors that drive defects and process inefficiencies.

- ➢ **Hypothesis Testing**: Conducting statistical tests to validate assumptions and identify relationships between variables. This analysis helps confirm the root causes of problems and guides the development of solutions.

- ➢ **Process Analysis**: Mapping the process in detail to identify bottlenecks, redundancies, and areas of waste. This analysis provides insights into process flow and highlights opportunities for improvement.

Improve

In the Improve phase, solutions are developed and implemented to address the root causes identified in the Analyze phase. This phase focuses on optimizing the process and achieving measurable improvements. Key activities in this phase include:

- ➢ **Solution Development**: Brainstorming and evaluating potential solutions to address root causes. This step involves selecting the most effective solutions based on feasibility, impact, and cost.

- ➢ **Pilot Testing**: Implementing solutions on a small scale to test their effectiveness and refine them before full-scale deployment. Pilot testing helps validate the solutions and identify any unforeseen issues.

- ➢ **Implementation**: Rolling out solutions across the process, ensuring that changes are communicated effectively and supported by training and resources.

Control

The Control phase ensures that improvements are sustained over time and that the process remains stable and consistent. This phase focuses on establishing controls and monitoring systems to prevent regression. Key activities in this phase include:

- ➢ **Control Plan**: Developing a control plan that outlines the monitoring and measurement activities required to maintain process improvements. This plan includes key metrics, responsibilities, and review schedules.

- ➢ **Statistical Process Control (SPC)**: Implementing control charts and other SPC tools to monitor process performance and detect variations in real-time.
- ➢ **Documentation and Training**: Ensuring that process changes are documented and that employees are trained to understand and support the new process.

By following the DMAIC methodology, organizations can systematically improve processes, reduce defects, and enhance quality. Each phase of DMAIC builds on the previous one, creating a continuous cycle of improvement that drives operational excellence and customer satisfaction.

Detailed Exploration of Each Phase:

Goals, Tools, and Techniques Used in Each Phase

In this section, we delve deeper into each phase of the DMAIC methodology, exploring the specific goals, tools, and techniques that make DMAIC a powerful approach for process improvement. Each phase builds on the last, employing targeted strategies to achieve meaningful results.

Define Phase

Goals: The Define phase aims to clearly articulate the problem, set objectives, and align project goals with customer needs and business objectives. The focus is on establishing a strong foundation for the project.

Tools and Techniques:

- **Project Charter**: A document that defines the project scope, objectives, deliverables, timeline, and stakeholders. The project charter serves as a roadmap for the project team.
- **Voice of the Customer (VoC)**: Methods such as surveys, interviews, and focus groups to gather customer insights and identify Critical to Quality (CTQ) requirements.
- **SIPOC Diagram**: A high-level process map that outlines Suppliers, Inputs, Process, Outputs, and Customers. This tool helps visualize the process and its key elements.
- **Stakeholder Analysis**: Identifying and analyzing stakeholders to ensure their needs and expectations are considered throughout the project.

Measure Phase

Goals: The Measure phase focuses on quantifying the problem and establishing a baseline for current process performance. Accurate data collection is crucial for understanding the process and identifying areas for improvement.

Tools and Techniques:

- **Data Collection Plan**: A structured approach to gathering data, detailing what data will be collected, how, and by whom.
- **Process Capability Analysis**: Assessing the process's ability to meet specifications using metrics like Cp, Cpk, Pp, and Ppk. Cp (Process Capability Index)
- **Measurement System Analysis (MSA)**: Evaluating the accuracy and precision of the measurement system to ensure data reliability. Techniques include Gage R&R (Repeatability and Reproducibility).

- **Flowcharting**: Creating detailed process maps to visualize each step and identify potential points of variation or inefficiency.

Analyze Phase

Goals: The Analyze phase aims to identify the root causes of defects and process inefficiencies. This phase uses data analysis and statistical techniques to pinpoint factors contributing to variation.

Tools and Techniques:

- **Root Cause Analysis**: Techniques such as Fishbone Diagrams (Ishikawa) and the 5 Whys method to systematically explore underlying causes of problems.
- **Hypothesis Testing**: Statistical tests, such as t-tests and ANOVA, to validate assumptions and identify significant factors affecting process performance.
- **Pareto Analysis**: Using the Pareto Principle (80/20 rule) to prioritize the most significant causes of defects or issues.
- **Regression Analysis**: Evaluating relationships between variables to understand how changes in one factor might affect others.

Improve Phase

Goals: The Improve phase focuses on developing and implementing solutions to address the root causes identified. The goal is to optimize the process and achieve measurable improvements.

Tools and Techniques:

- **Brainstorming and Solution Generation**: Engaging team members in creative thinking to generate potential solutions.
- **Design of Experiments (DOE)**: Planning and conducting experiments to test the effects of changes on process performance.

- **Pilot Testing**: Implementing solutions on a small scale to validate effectiveness before full-scale deployment.
- **Process Redesign**: Making structural changes to the process to eliminate inefficiencies and enhance flow.

Control Phase

Goals: The Control phase ensures that process improvements are sustained over time. The focus is on implementing controls and monitoring systems to prevent regression and maintain process stability.

Tools and Techniques:

- **Control Plan**: A document detailing monitoring activities, responsibilities, and review schedules to sustain improvements.
- **Statistical Process Control (SPC)**: Using control charts to monitor process performance and detect variations in real-time.
- **Standard Operating Procedures (SOPs)**: Documenting process changes and ensuring all team members understand and follow the new procedures.
- **Training and Communication**: Providing ongoing training and communication to support the new process and foster a culture of continuous improvement.

By understanding the goals, tools, and techniques used in each phase of DMAIC, organizations can effectively navigate the process improvement journey and achieve sustainable results. This detailed exploration provides a roadmap for practitioners, equipping them with the knowledge and skills needed to lead successful Six Sigma projects.

Case Study:

A Real-World Example of a Successful DMAIC Project

To illustrate the power and effectiveness of the DMAIC methodology, let's explore a real-world case study of a successful Six Sigma project undertaken by a manufacturing company. This project highlights the practical application of each phase of DMAIC and demonstrates the tangible benefits of Six Sigma in process improvement.

Background

A leading automotive parts manufacturer was experiencing high defect rates in its brake pad production line, resulting in increased scrap costs and customer dissatisfaction. The company decided to implement a Six Sigma project using the DMAIC methodology to address these issues and enhance product quality.

Define Phase

In the Define phase, the project team set out to clearly define the problem and establish objectives. The project charter was developed, outlining the scope, goals, and deliverables of the project. The primary objective was to reduce the defect rate in the brake pad production process from 8% to less than 2%, thereby improving customer satisfaction and reducing costs.

The team conducted Voice of the Customer (VoC) analysis, gathering feedback from key customers to understand their quality expectations and requirements. The SIPOC diagram was created to map the high-level process flow, identifying key inputs, outputs, and stakeholders involved in the production process.

Measure Phase

During the Measure phase, the team focused on collecting accurate data to establish a baseline for the current process performance. A comprehensive data collection plan was developed, specifying the data sources, collection methods, and measurement tools.

The team conducted a Process Capability Analysis to assess the process's ability to meet specifications. The analysis revealed significant variation in the production process, contributing to the high defect rate.

Measurement System Analysis (MSA) was performed to ensure the accuracy and reliability of the measurement system.

Analyze Phase

In the Analyze phase, the team used data analysis and statistical tools to identify the root causes of defects. Root Cause Analysis was conducted using Fishbone Diagrams and the 5 Whys method, revealing that inconsistencies in material quality and machine calibration were major contributors to defects.

The team also employed Hypothesis Testing and Pareto Analysis to validate assumptions and prioritize the most significant causes of defects. Regression Analysis was used to explore relationships between variables, providing insights into how changes in material quality and machine settings affected process performance.

Improve Phase

The Improve phase focused on developing and implementing solutions to address the identified root causes. The team engaged in brainstorming sessions to generate potential solutions and conducted Design of Experiments (DOE) to test the effects of proposed changes on process performance.

Key improvements included implementing stricter quality control measures for incoming materials, enhancing machine calibration procedures, and providing additional training for operators. Pilot testing was conducted to validate the effectiveness of these solutions before full-scale implementation.

Control Phase

In the Control phase, the team implemented controls to sustain the improvements achieved. A Control Plan was developed, outlining monitoring activities, responsibilities, and review schedules. Statistical Process Control (SPC) was introduced, utilizing control charts to monitor process performance and detect variations in real-time.

Standard Operating Procedures (SOPs) were updated to reflect process changes, and ongoing training and communication ensured that all team members understood and adhered to the new procedures. Regular audits and reviews were conducted to maintain process stability and prevent regression.

Results

The successful implementation of the DMAIC project led to a significant reduction in the defect rate, from 8% to less than 1.5%, exceeding the project's original objectives. The company achieved substantial cost savings through reduced scrap and rework, and customer satisfaction improved due to the enhanced quality of brake pads.

This case study demonstrates the practical application of the DMAIC methodology in a real-world setting, showcasing the transformative impact of Six Sigma on process performance and quality. By following the structured approach of DMAIC, the company was able to identify and eliminate root causes of defects, optimize processes, and achieve sustainable improvements.

Chapter 3: Understanding DMADV

Overview of DMADV

Define Phase

The Define phase establishes the foundation for the project by clearly outlining its objectives, scope, and goals. This phase focuses on understanding the customer's needs and identifying the problem or opportunity for improvement.

- **Objectives**: Define what the project aims to achieve, including specific and measurable goals.
- **Scope**: Determine the boundaries of the project, ensuring that it is manageable and focused.
- **Customer Requirements**: Identify and document the Voice of the Customer (VOC) to understand their needs and expectations.
- **Project Charter**: Create a project charter to formalize the project, outlining roles, responsibilities, and timelines.

Measure Phase

In the Measure phase, the focus is on collecting data and establishing baselines for current process performance. This phase involves gathering information on existing processes and understanding their limitations.

- **Data Collection**: Develop a detailed plan for collecting relevant data, ensuring accuracy and consistency.

- **Baseline Measurement**: Establish current performance baselines to identify gaps between current capabilities and customer requirements.
- **Quality Function Deployment (QFD)**: Use QFD tools to translate customer requirements into technical specifications.

Analyze Phase

The Analyze phase involves examining the collected data to identify root causes of process inefficiencies and potential solutions. This phase focuses on understanding the relationships between variables and uncovering opportunities for improvement.

- **Root Cause Analysis**: Utilize techniques like fishbone diagrams or 5 Whys to identify underlying causes of issues.
- **Process Mapping**: Create detailed process maps to visualize workflow and identify bottlenecks or redundancies.
- **Design Alternatives**: Develop and evaluate alternative solutions based on analysis findings.

Design Phase

In the Design phase, the team develops detailed plans for the new process or product. This phase focuses on creating solutions that align with customer requirements and address the issues identified in previous phases.

- **Prototyping**: Create prototypes or models to test potential solutions and gather feedback.
- **Design for Six Sigma (DFSS)**: Implement DFSS principles to ensure that designs meet Six Sigma quality standards.
- **Simulation**: Use simulation tools to model the performance of the new design under different scenarios.

Verify Phase

The Verify phase ensures that the new process or product meets the desired quality standards and customer requirements. This phase involves testing and validating the design before full-scale implementation.

- ➤ **Pilot Testing**: Conduct pilot tests to validate the design and identify any final adjustments needed.
- ➤ **Performance Measurement**: Develop metrics to monitor the performance of the new process and ensure it meets specifications.
- ➤ **Implementation Plan**: Create a detailed plan for rolling out the new design, including training, documentation, and support.

The DMADV methodology provides a structured approach for designing new processes or products that meet customer needs and achieve high-quality standards. Each phase builds on the previous one, ensuring a thorough understanding of customer requirements and careful planning and execution of the design. By following the DMADV framework, organizations can innovate and improve their processes, leading to increased customer satisfaction and competitive advantage.

Detailed Exploration of Each Phase

Define Phase

Goals:

The primary goal of the Define phase is to establish a clear understanding of the project objectives, customer needs, and scope. This phase sets the direction for the entire project by identifying what success looks like and aligning the team around a shared vision.

Tools and Techniques:

- ➤ **Project Charter**: A document that outlines the project goals, scope, roles, responsibilities, and timeline. It serves as a guiding reference for the team.

- **Voice of the Customer (VOC)**: Techniques such as surveys, interviews, and focus groups are used to gather customer feedback and requirements.
- **Stakeholder Analysis**: Identifying and understanding the needs and influence of stakeholders to ensure their expectations are met.
- **Critical to Quality (CTQ) Trees**: A tool to translate broad customer needs into specific, measurable requirements.

Measure Phase

Goals:
The Measure phase aims to collect accurate data and establish baseline performance metrics. This phase focuses on understanding current process capabilities and identifying any gaps between existing performance and customer requirements.

Tools and Techniques:

- **Data Collection Plan**: A structured approach to gathering necessary data, detailing what, how, and by whom the data will be collected.
- **Quality Function Deployment (QFD)**: A tool to translate customer requirements into technical specifications and prioritize them based on importance.
- **Baseline Measurement**: Establishing initial performance metrics to compare against future improvements.
- **Process Mapping**: Creating visual representations of current processes to identify inefficiencies and areas for improvement.

Analyze Phase

Goals:
The Analyze phase focuses on examining the data to uncover root causes of process inefficiencies and identifying potential improvement opportunities. This phase is crucial for understanding the relationships between variables and pinpointing areas that need redesign.

Tools and Techniques:

- **Root Cause Analysis**: Techniques like fishbone diagrams, 5 Whys, and Pareto analysis to identify underlying causes of issues.
- **Process Capability Analysis**: Assessing the ability of current processes to meet specifications using metrics like Cp, Cpk, Pp, and Ppk.
- **Design of Experiments (DOE)**: Planning and conducting experiments to study the effects of multiple variables on process performance.
- **Failure Mode and Effects Analysis (FMEA)**: Identifying potential failure points in the process and assessing their impact on quality.

Design Phase

Goals:

The Design phase aims to develop detailed plans for the new process or product, ensuring that it aligns with customer requirements and addresses identified issues. This phase involves creating and testing prototypes to refine the design.

Tools and Techniques:

- **Prototyping**: Creating physical or digital models to test potential solutions and gather feedback.
- **Design for Six Sigma (DFSS)**: Implementing DFSS principles to ensure designs meet Six Sigma quality standards and are robust against variations.
- **Simulation**: Using software tools to model the performance of the new design under different scenarios and identify potential improvements.
- **Value Engineering**: Analyzing the design to ensure it delivers the best value by balancing cost, quality, and functionality.

Verify Phase

Goals:
The Verify phase ensures that the new process or product meets the desired quality standards and customer requirements. This phase involves rigorous testing and validation to confirm the effectiveness of the design before full-scale implementation.

Tools and Techniques:

- ➤ **Pilot Testing**: Conducting small-scale tests to validate the design and identify any final adjustments needed.
- ➤ **Control Plans**: Developing plans to monitor and control the performance of the new process, ensuring it consistently meets specifications.
- ➤ **Statistical Process Control (SPC)**: Using control charts and other statistical tools to monitor process stability and performance over time.
- ➤ **Customer Feedback**: Gathering feedback from customers to verify that the new design meets their needs and expectations.

The DMADV methodology provides a comprehensive framework for designing high-quality processes and products. By focusing on clear goals and using a variety of tools and techniques, each phase builds on the previous one to ensure a thorough understanding of customer requirements and careful planning and execution of the design. This approach enables organizations to innovate and improve their processes, leading to increased customer satisfaction and competitive advantage.

Case Study:
Implementing DMADV in a Financial Services Company

Background

A leading financial services company sought to develop a new online loan application process to improve customer satisfaction and reduce application processing time. The existing process was cumbersome and resulted in frequent customer complaints about delays and errors. The company decided to implement the DMADV methodology to design a streamlined, customer-centric process.

Define Phase

Goals: The team aimed to create a new online loan application process that was user-friendly, efficient, and met customer expectations.

Actions Taken:

- Conducted surveys and focus groups to gather customer feedback and identify key pain points.
- Developed a project charter outlining objectives, scope, and timelines.
- Identified critical customer requirements, such as fast approval times and intuitive navigation, using Critical to Quality (CTQ) Trees.

Measure Phase

Goals: Establish baseline metrics for current process performance and understand customer needs.

Actions Taken:

- Created a detailed data collection plan to gather information on existing application times and error rates.
- Used Quality Function Deployment (QFD) to translate customer requirements into technical specifications.
- Established baseline measurements, revealing that the average application processing time was seven days with a 15% error rate.

Analyze Phase

Goals: Identify root causes of inefficiencies and potential improvements.

Actions Taken:

- Conducted root cause analysis using fishbone diagrams and identified key issues, such as outdated software and complex application forms.
- Performed process mapping to visualize current workflows and identify bottlenecks.
- Conducted a process capability analysis, finding that the process could not consistently meet customer expectations.

Design Phase

Goals: Develop a new, streamlined loan application process that meets customer requirements.

Actions Taken:

- Created prototypes of the new online application interface and tested them with customer focus groups.
- Implemented Design for Six Sigma (DFSS) principles to ensure the new process was robust and met quality standards.
- Used simulation tools to model the new process, identifying potential improvements and validating design decisions.

Verify Phase

Goals: Ensure the new process meets quality standards and customer requirements.

Actions Taken:

- Conducted pilot testing with a select group of customers to validate the new process and gather feedback.
- Developed control plans to monitor the new process's performance and ensure consistent quality.
- Implemented Statistical Process Control (SPC) tools to track performance metrics, such as processing time and error rates.

Results

The implementation of the DMADV methodology led to a significant improvement in the loan application process. The average processing time was reduced from seven days to two days, and the error rate dropped from 15% to 2%. Customer satisfaction increased, with surveys indicating a 30% improvement in customer approval ratings for the application process. The new process not only met but exceeded customer expectations, demonstrating the effectiveness of the DMADV approach in designing high-quality, customer-centric solutions.

This case study illustrates the power of the DMADV methodology in driving process innovation and improvement. By systematically defining, measuring, analyzing, designing, and verifying the new loan application process, the financial services company was able to achieve substantial gains in efficiency and customer satisfaction. This success underscores the value of DMADV in developing processes that align with customer needs and deliver superior performance.

Chapter 4: Tools and Techniques for DMAIC

Data Collection and Analysis in DMAIC

Measure Phase: Data Collection Tools

The Measure phase focuses on collecting accurate data to establish a baseline for current process performance. Effective data collection ensures the reliability of subsequent analysis.

Goals:

- Establish baseline metrics for process performance.
- Ensure accurate and consistent data collection.
- Identify key performance indicators (KPIs).

Tools and Techniques:

1. **Data Collection Plan**: A structured approach detailing what data will be collected, how, by whom, and the frequency. It ensures that data collection is systematic and consistent.

2. **Check Sheets**: Simple forms used to collect data in real time at the location where the data is generated. Check sheets are useful for capturing frequency counts of specific events or defects.

3. **Surveys and Questionnaires**: Tools for gathering qualitative data from stakeholders, customers, or employees. These tools help in understanding perceptions, opinions, and experiences related to the process.

4. **Sampling Methods**: Techniques such as random sampling, stratified sampling, or systematic sampling are used to select

representative data sets for analysis. Sampling reduces the time and cost of data collection while ensuring accuracy.

5. **Measurement System Analysis (MSA)**: An evaluation of the measurement system's accuracy and precision, ensuring that data collected is reliable. Techniques include Gage R&R (Repeatability and Reproducibility) studies.

Analyze Phase: Data Analysis Tools

The Analyze phase involves examining the collected data to identify root causes of process inefficiencies and opportunities for improvement. This phase is critical for understanding the relationships between variables and determining areas for process optimization.

Goals:

- Identify root causes of problems and inefficiencies.
- Understand process performance and variability.
- Develop potential solutions based on data insights.

Tools and Techniques:

1. **Descriptive Statistics**: Techniques such as mean, median, mode, standard deviation, and range provide a summary of the data, helping to understand the central tendency and variability.

2. **Pareto Analysis**: A graphical tool based on the Pareto principle (80/20 rule), used to identify the most significant factors contributing to a problem. It helps prioritize areas for improvement.

3. **Cause and Effect Diagrams (Fishbone Diagrams)**: Visual tools used to identify potential root causes of a problem by categorizing factors affecting a process. They help in systematically analyzing complex issues.

4. **Histogram**: A graphical representation of data distribution, useful for identifying patterns, trends, and outliers. Histograms help visualize process performance and variability.

5. **Scatter Plots**: Graphical tools used to examine the relationship between two variables. Scatter plots help identify correlations and potential causal relationships.

6. **Regression Analysis**: A statistical technique for quantifying the relationship between variables and predicting future outcomes. Regression analysis helps in understanding how changes in one variable affect others.

7. **Process Capability Analysis**: Techniques like Cp, Cpk, Pp, and Ppk are used to assess the process's ability to meet specifications and identify areas for improvement.

8. **Hypothesis Testing**: Statistical tests (e.g., t-tests, ANOVA) used to validate assumptions and determine the significance of observed differences in data. Hypothesis testing helps in making data-driven decisions.

Effective data collection and analysis are fundamental to the success of the DMAIC methodology. By employing these tools in the Measure and Analyze phases, organizations can gain valuable insights into process performance, identify root causes of inefficiencies, and develop targeted solutions for improvement. This systematic approach ensures that decisions are based on accurate and reliable data, leading to more effective process optimization and increased operational efficiency.

Problem-Solving Techniques in DMAIC

Analyze Phase: Identifying Root Causes

The Analyze phase focuses on understanding the underlying causes of process problems. Identifying root causes is essential for developing targeted and effective solutions.

Goals:

- ➢ Determine the root causes of process inefficiencies.
- ➢ Understand the factors contributing to variability and defects.
- ➢ Prioritize issues based on impact and feasibility of solutions.

Tools and Techniques:

1. **Cause and Effect Diagrams (Fishbone or Ishikawa Diagrams)**: Visual tools that help identify potential root causes of a problem by categorizing factors into major categories such as people, methods, materials, and environment. They facilitate systematic analysis and brainstorming.

2. **5 Whys Analysis**: A simple, iterative technique that involves asking "why" repeatedly to drill down to the root cause of a problem. It encourages critical thinking and helps uncover underlying issues.

3. **Pareto Analysis**: Based on the Pareto principle (80/20 rule), this tool helps identify the most significant factors contributing to a problem. It prioritizes issues by highlighting the vital few causes that need attention.

4. **Failure Mode and Effects Analysis (FMEA)**: A proactive tool used to identify potential failure modes, their effects, and causes. It assesses the risk associated with each failure mode and prioritizes them for corrective action based on severity, occurrence, and detection ratings.

5. **Scatter Plots**: Graphical tools used to explore relationships between two variables. They help identify potential correlations and causal links, providing insights into process variability.

Improve Phase: Developing Potential Solutions

The Improve phase focuses on developing and implementing solutions to address root causes and improve process performance.

Goals:

- Generate innovative and effective solutions to address identified root causes.
- Evaluate and prioritize solutions based on impact and feasibility.
- Implement changes that lead to measurable improvements.

Tools and Techniques:

1. **Brainstorming**: A creative problem-solving technique that encourages team members to generate a wide range of ideas without criticism. It fosters innovation and encourages diverse perspectives.

2. **Affinity Diagrams**: A tool used to organize and categorize ideas generated during brainstorming sessions. It helps identify patterns and themes, making it easier to develop coherent solutions.

3. **Design of Experiments (DOE)**: A statistical approach used to plan, conduct, and analyze controlled experiments. DOE helps identify optimal solutions by understanding the effects of multiple variables on process performance.

4. **Pilot Testing**: Implementing solutions on a small scale to validate their effectiveness before full-scale deployment. Pilot testing helps identify any potential issues and refine solutions.

5. **PDCA Cycle (Plan-Do-Check-Act)**: A continuous improvement cycle used to implement and refine solutions. It emphasizes planning changes, testing them, evaluating results, and making necessary adjustments.

6. **Kaizen**: A philosophy of continuous improvement that involves small, incremental changes to processes. Kaizen encourages ongoing evaluation and refinement to achieve long-term improvements.

Problem-solving techniques are integral to the success of the DMAIC methodology. By employing these tools in the Analyze and Improve phases, organizations can effectively identify root causes, develop targeted solutions, and implement changes that lead to sustainable process improvements. This structured approach ensures that problems are addressed systematically and solutions are based on data-driven insights, leading to enhanced process performance and increased efficiency.

Implementing Improvements in DMAIC

Improve Phase: Piloting Improvements

The Improve phase focuses on developing and implementing solutions to address identified root causes. Piloting improvements is a crucial step to validate their effectiveness before full-scale deployment.

Goals:

- Test and validate solutions on a small scale.
- Identify potential issues and make necessary adjustments.
- Gather data to support decision-making for full-scale implementation.

Techniques for Piloting Improvements:

1. **Pilot Testing**: Conducting small-scale trials to test the feasibility and effectiveness of proposed solutions. Pilot testing helps identify any unforeseen challenges and provides an opportunity to refine solutions before full-scale implementation.

2. **Simulation**: Using software tools to model the performance of proposed solutions in a controlled environment. Simulation allows teams to test different scenarios and assess potential outcomes without disrupting actual operations.

3. **Prototyping**: Creating physical or digital models of new processes or products to test their functionality and gather

feedback. Prototyping helps identify design flaws and allows for iterative refinement.

4. **Feedback Loops**: Establishing mechanisms for collecting feedback from stakeholders during the pilot phase. Feedback loops provide valuable insights into the effectiveness of solutions and highlight areas for improvement.

Control Phase: Refining and Sustaining Improvements

The Control phase ensures that improvements are sustained over time and that the process remains stable and efficient. This phase involves monitoring performance and making necessary adjustments to maintain gains.

Goals:

- Ensure that improvements are effectively integrated into existing processes.
- Monitor performance to prevent regression.
- Continuously refine solutions to optimize performance.

Techniques for Refining and Sustaining Improvements:

1. **Control Plans**: Developing detailed plans to monitor and control the performance of the improved process. Control plans outline key metrics, data collection methods, and response strategies for deviations.

2. **Statistical Process Control (SPC)**: Using control charts and other statistical tools to monitor process stability and detect variations. SPC helps identify trends, shifts, and potential issues before they impact performance.

3. **Standard Operating Procedures (SOPs)**: Documenting new processes and procedures to ensure consistency and adherence to best practices. SOPs provide clear guidelines for employees and help maintain process quality.

4. **Training and Communication**: Providing training to employees on new processes and fostering open communication to encourage feedback and suggestions. Training ensures that staff are equipped to implement improvements effectively.

5. **Continuous Improvement**: Encouraging a culture of ongoing evaluation and refinement through techniques like Kaizen and the PDCA cycle. Continuous improvement fosters innovation and helps sustain long-term gains.

Implementing, piloting, and refining improvements are critical components of the DMAIC methodology. By using these techniques, organizations can validate solutions, ensure successful integration, and maintain process improvements over time. This structured approach leads to sustainable enhancements in performance, efficiency, and customer satisfaction, driving long-term success.

Chapter 5:
Tools and Techniques for DMADV

Design and Innovation Tools in DMADV

Design Phase: Creating Innovative Solutions

The Design phase focuses on developing detailed plans for new processes or products. This phase emphasizes creativity and innovation to ensure that solutions align with customer needs and address identified issues.

Goals:

- Develop creative and effective solutions to meet customer requirements.
- Translate customer needs into technical specifications and design features.
- Ensure designs are robust, reliable, and scalable.

Tools and Techniques for Design and Innovation:

1. Quality Function Deployment (QFD): A structured approach to translating customer needs into specific technical requirements. QFD prioritizes customer requirements and ensures that design decisions align with those needs.

2. Design Thinking: A human-centered approach to innovation that emphasizes empathy, ideation, and prototyping. Design thinking involves understanding user needs, generating creative ideas, and testing solutions through rapid prototyping.

3. TRIZ (Theory of Inventive Problem Solving): A methodology for systematic innovation that leverages patterns of invention from various fields. TRIZ provides tools and techniques to solve complex problems and generate innovative solutions.

4. Morphological Analysis: A technique for exploring all possible solutions to a problem by breaking it down into its component parts and examining the combinations. This approach fosters creativity and innovation by considering a wide range of possibilities.

5. Brainstorming: A collaborative technique that encourages team members to generate a wide range of ideas without judgment. Brainstorming fosters creativity and leverages diverse perspectives to develop innovative solutions.

6. Mind Mapping: A visual tool that helps organize and explore ideas by creating a diagram of thoughts and connections. Mind mapping supports creative thinking and helps uncover new insights and opportunities.

7. Benchmarking: Comparing processes, products, or services against industry standards or best practices to identify areas for improvement and innovation. Benchmarking provides valuable insights and inspiration for developing superior designs.

8. Prototyping and Iteration: Creating physical or digital models of proposed solutions to test their functionality and gather feedback. Prototyping allows for iterative refinement, enabling teams to develop and enhance designs based on user input.

9. Value Engineering: Analyzing design features to ensure they deliver maximum value by balancing cost, quality, and functionality. Value engineering involves evaluating design options and making trade-offs to optimize performance.

10. Simulation and Modeling: Using software tools to simulate the performance of proposed designs under different scenarios. Simulation helps identify potential issues and optimize designs before implementation.

Design and innovation tools are integral to the success of the Design phase in the DMADV methodology. By employing these techniques, organizations can develop creative and effective solutions that meet customer requirements and achieve high-quality standards. This structured approach ensures that designs are robust, reliable, and aligned with customer needs, leading to improved products and processes and increased customer satisfaction.

Verification and Validation in DMADV

Verify Phase: Ensuring Design Effectiveness

The Verify phase focuses on confirming that the design meets the desired quality standards and customer requirements. This phase involves rigorous testing and validation to ensure the solution's effectiveness before full-scale implementation.

Goals:

- ➢ Validate that the design meets customer and business requirements.
- ➢ Identify and resolve any issues before full-scale deployment.
- ➢ Ensure that the solution delivers the intended benefits and performance.

Tools and Techniques for Verification and Validation:

1. **Design Reviews**: Structured evaluations of the design to ensure it meets specifications and requirements. Design reviews involve cross-functional teams who assess the design's feasibility, functionality, and alignment with customer needs.

2. **Prototyping and Testing**: Developing physical or digital prototypes to test the design's functionality and gather feedback. Testing helps identify potential issues and allows for iterative refinement based on user input.

3. **Pilot Testing**: Conducting small-scale trials of the design to validate its performance and effectiveness. Pilot testing provides real-world insights into the design's capabilities and identifies areas for improvement.

4. **Simulation and Modeling**: Using software tools to simulate the design's performance under various conditions. Simulation helps identify potential issues and optimize the design before implementation.

5. **Failure Mode and Effects Analysis (FMEA)**: Identifying potential failure modes and assessing their impact on the design's performance. FMEA helps prioritize risks and develop mitigation strategies to ensure reliability.

6. **Statistical Process Control (SPC)**: Using control charts and other statistical tools to monitor the design's stability and performance. SPC helps identify trends and variations, ensuring the design meets quality standards.

7. **Acceptance Testing**: Conducting tests to verify that the design meets predefined criteria and specifications. Acceptance testing involves end-users and stakeholders to ensure the solution meets their expectations.

8. **Quality Assurance (QA) Audits**: Independent assessments of the design process and output to ensure compliance with quality standards. QA audits provide an objective evaluation of the design's effectiveness and identify areas for improvement.

9. **Customer Feedback**: Gathering input from customers and stakeholders to verify that the design meets their needs and expectations. Customer feedback provides valuable insights for refining and optimizing the design.

10. **Traceability Matrix**: A tool that maps customer requirements to design features and testing activities. The traceability matrix

ensures that all requirements are addressed and validated through testing.

Verification and validation tools are crucial for ensuring that designs meet customer and business needs in the DMADV methodology. By employing these techniques in the Verify phase, organizations can confirm the effectiveness of their designs, identify and resolve issues, and ensure that solutions deliver the intended benefits. This structured approach leads to successful implementation and increased customer satisfaction, driving long-term success and competitive advantage.

Case Study: Developing a New Mobile Banking Application

Background

A leading bank sought to develop a new mobile banking application to enhance customer experience and increase market share in the digital banking sector. The existing application was outdated and lacked essential features, leading to customer dissatisfaction and increased competition. The bank decided to implement the DMADV methodology to design a user-friendly, secure, and feature-rich application that would meet customer needs and improve engagement.

Define Phase

Goals: Establish a clear understanding of customer needs and project objectives to guide the development of the new mobile banking application.

Actions Taken:

- ➤ Conducted surveys and interviews with customers to gather feedback on the existing application and identify desired features.
- ➤ Developed a project charter outlining objectives, scope, timelines, and roles and responsibilities.

- Identified critical customer requirements, such as ease of use, security, real-time notifications, and personalized insights, using Quality Function Deployment (QFD).

Measure Phase

Goals: Gather data to establish baselines for current application performance and customer expectations.

Actions Taken:

- Developed a data collection plan to gather quantitative and qualitative data on current application usage, performance metrics, and customer feedback.
- Used bench marking to compare the bank's application with competitors and industry standards, identifying gaps and opportunities for improvement.
- Established baseline measurements, such as average session duration, transaction success rate, and customer satisfaction scores.

Analyze Phase

Goals: Identify root causes of existing application issues and potential areas for innovation and improvement.

Actions Taken:

- Conducted root cause analysis using fishbone diagrams and identified key issues, such as slow performance, limited features, and complex navigation.
- Performed process mapping to understand user journeys and identify bottlenecks and pain points.
- Utilized TRIZ (Theory of Inventive Problem Solving) to explore innovative solutions and features that could differentiate the new application.

Design Phase

Goals: Develop a detailed design for the new mobile banking application that aligns with customer needs and addresses identified issues.

Actions Taken:

- Used Design Thinking workshops to brainstorm and develop creative solutions, focusing on user-centered design principles.
- Created wire frames and prototypes to test user interfaces and gather feedback from customers and stakeholders.
- Implemented Value Engineering to balance cost, quality, and functionality, ensuring the design delivered maximum value to customers.

Verify Phase

Goals: Validate that the new application design meets customer and business requirements and is ready for full-scale implementation.

Actions Taken:

- Conducted pilot testing with a select group of customers to validate the application's performance and gather feedback.
- Used simulation tools to model the application's performance under various conditions and identify potential issues.
- Performed acceptance testing with end-users to ensure the application met predefined criteria and customer expectations.
- Gathered customer feedback to verify that the application delivered the desired features and user experience.

Results

The implementation of the DMADV methodology led to the successful development of a new mobile banking application that exceeded customer expectations. The application featured a streamlined user interface, enhanced security measures, real-time notifications, and personalized financial insights. Customer satisfaction scores increased by 40%, and the application saw a 50% increase in usage within the first six months of launch. The new application strengthened the bank's competitive position in the digital banking sector and demonstrated the effectiveness of the DMADV approach in developing innovative and customer-centric solutions.

This case study illustrates the power of the DMADV methodology in developing new products and services that align with customer needs and business goals. By systematically defining, measuring, analyzing, designing, and verifying the new mobile banking application, the bank was able to achieve substantial improvements in customer satisfaction and engagement. This success underscores the value of DMADV in driving innovation and delivering high-quality solutions in today's competitive market.

Chapter 6:
Integrating DMAIC and DMADV in Business Strategy

Aligning Six Sigma with Business Goals

The Importance of Alignment

Aligning Six Sigma projects with business goals is crucial for maximizing the impact of process improvements on the organization's overall strategy. This alignment ensures that resources are focused on initiatives that drive strategic objectives, enhance competitiveness, and deliver measurable value.

Goals:

- Ensure Six Sigma projects support and advance strategic business objectives.
- Maximize the return on investment (ROI) from Six Sigma initiatives.
- Foster a culture of continuous improvement that aligns with the organization's mission and vision

Strategies for Aligning Six Sigma Projects

1. **Understand Strategic Objectives**: Begin by clearly understanding the organization's mission, vision, and strategic goals. This understanding provides a framework for identifying Six Sigma projects that can contribute to these objectives.

2. **Identify Key Performance Indicators (KPIs)**: Define KPIs that align with strategic goals and use them to measure the

success of Six Sigma projects. KPIs provide a quantifiable way to assess the impact of process improvements on business performance.

3. **Conduct Strategic Assessments**: Regularly assess the organization's strategic priorities and identify areas where Six Sigma can add value. Use tools like SWOT analysis (Strengths, Weaknesses, Opportunities, Threats) to identify opportunities for improvement.

4. **Select High-Impact Projects**: Prioritize Six Sigma projects based on their potential impact on strategic goals. Focus on projects that address critical pain points, enhance customer satisfaction, and drive operational efficiency.

5. **Involve Leadership**: Engage senior leaders and executives in the selection and prioritization of Six Sigma projects. Leadership involvement ensures that projects are aligned with strategic priorities and receive the necessary support and resources.

6. **Integrate Six Sigma into Strategic Planning**: Incorporate Six Sigma methodologies into the organization's strategic planning process. Use DMAIC and DMADV frameworks to identify and address strategic challenges and opportunities.

7. **Communicate Alignment**: Clearly communicate the alignment between Six Sigma projects and business goals to all stakeholders. Regular updates on project progress and outcomes help reinforce the strategic relevance of Six Sigma initiatives.

8. **Foster a Culture of Continuous Improvement**: Cultivate a culture that encourages continuous improvement and innovation. Aligning Six Sigma with business goals fosters a mindset of proactive problem-solving and strategic thinking.

9. **Measure and Report Outcomes**: Use KPIs and other metrics to measure the success of Six Sigma projects and their alignment with business goals. Regular reporting on project outcomes helps demonstrate the value of Six Sigma to the organization.

10. **Adjust and Adapt**: Be prepared to adjust Six Sigma projects as business goals evolve. Flexibility ensures that projects remain relevant and continue to support the organization's strategic direction.

Aligning Six Sigma projects with business goals is essential for ensuring that process improvements drive strategic success. By integrating Six Sigma into the organization's strategic planning and prioritizing projects based on their impact on business objectives, companies can maximize the value of their Six Sigma initiatives. This alignment fosters a culture of continuous improvement and innovation, positioning the organization for long-term success and competitive advantage.

Selecting the Right Projects for DMAIC and DMADV

Importance of Project Selection

Choosing the right projects is crucial for the success of Six Sigma initiatives. Proper project selection ensures that efforts are focused on high-impact areas, resources are used efficiently, and outcomes align with business goals.

Goals:

- Identify projects that offer significant potential for improvement and value creation.
- Ensure alignment with organizational goals and strategic priorities.
- Maximize the return on investment (ROI) of Six Sigma initiatives.

Criteria for Selecting DMAIC Projects

DMAIC projects are best suited for improving existing processes. The following criteria can help identify suitable DMAIC projects:

1. **Process Performance Issues**: Select processes with known performance issues, such as high defect rates, inefficiencies, or customer complaints. DMAIC is ideal for addressing these problems and optimizing process performance.

2. **Data Availability**: Ensure that sufficient data is available to analyze the process and identify root causes. Access to accurate data is critical for the success of DMAIC projects.

3. **Clear Improvement Potential**: Choose projects where the potential for improvement is clear and measurable. This includes reducing defects, improving cycle times, or enhancing customer satisfaction.

4. **Cost-Effectiveness**: Evaluate the potential cost savings or revenue enhancements resulting from the project. Select projects with a favorable cost-benefit ratio.

5. **Alignment with Business Goals**: Ensure that the project aligns with the organization's strategic objectives and addresses key priorities.

6. **Stakeholder Support**: Confirm that stakeholders, including management and team members, support the project. Stakeholder buy-in is crucial for successful implementation.

7. **Feasibility and Complexity**: Consider the feasibility and complexity of the project. Select projects that are manageable within the organization's resources and capabilities.

8. **Criteria for Selecting DMADV Projects:** DMADV projects are suitable for designing new processes or products. The following criteria can help identify suitable DMADV projects:

9. **New Product or Process Development**: Choose projects that involve developing new products, services, or processes where no existing solution meets customer needs.

10. **Customer Requirements**: Select projects that focus on meeting specific customer requirements or addressing unmet needs. DMADV is ideal for designing solutions that align with customer expectations.

11. **Market or Competitive Pressures**: Consider projects driven by market demands or competitive pressures that require innovative solutions to stay ahead.

12. **Strategic Initiatives**: Align projects with strategic initiatives that involve significant change or innovation, such as entering new markets or launching new product lines.

13. **Technology or Innovation Opportunities**: Identify projects that leverage new technologies or innovations to create value and differentiation.

14. **Risk and Uncertainty**: Assess the level of risk and uncertainty involved in the project. DMADV is well-suited for projects where risks can be mitigated through careful design and validation.

15. **Resource Availability**: Ensure that resources, including time, budget, and expertise, are available to support the project.

Selecting the right projects is a critical step in the success of Six Sigma initiatives. By carefully evaluating criteria for DMAIC and DMADV projects, organizations can focus on high-impact areas that align with business goals and deliver meaningful improvements. This strategic approach ensures that resources are used effectively, leading to enhanced process performance, customer satisfaction, and competitive advantage.

Balancing Resources and Priorities in Six Sigma

The Challenge of Managing Multiple Projects

Managing multiple Six Sigma projects simultaneously can be challenging, especially when resources are limited and priorities compete. Effective resource and priority management are crucial for ensuring that projects deliver value and align with organizational objectives.

Goals:

- Optimize resource allocation to maximize project impact.
- Prioritize projects based on strategic importance and potential benefits.
- Ensure timely completion of projects without overextending resources.

Strategies for Managing Multiple Six Sigma Projects

1. **Establish Clear Priorities**: Begin by identifying strategic priorities and aligning Six Sigma projects with these objectives. Prioritize projects that offer the most significant potential for impact and value creation.

2. **Develop a Project Portfolio**: Create a project portfolio that provides a comprehensive overview of all Six Sigma initiatives. The portfolio should include project goals, timelines, resource requirements, and expected outcomes.

3. **Resource Allocation Planning**: Develop a resource allocation plan that ensures the optimal distribution of resources, including personnel, budget, and technology, across all projects. Consider using project management software to track and manage resource allocation.

4. **Use a Project Management Framework**: Implement a project management framework, such as Agile or Lean, to manage project workflows and ensure efficient use of resources. This framework provides structure and consistency in project execution.

5. **Regularly Review and Adjust Priorities**: Conduct regular reviews of project priorities and progress to ensure alignment with strategic goals. Be prepared to adjust priorities based on changing business needs and resource availability.

6. **Balance Short-Term and Long-Term Goals**: Balance projects that deliver short-term gains with those that contribute to long-term strategic objectives. This balance ensures that the organization remains agile and responsive to immediate needs while pursuing sustained growth.

7. **Effective Communication and Collaboration**: Foster open communication and collaboration among project teams to share resources, knowledge, and best practices. This approach helps prevent resource bottlenecks and encourages innovative solutions.

8. **Monitor Key Performance Indicators (KPIs)**: Establish KPIs to measure the performance and progress of each project. Regularly monitor KPIs to identify potential issues and make data-driven decisions regarding resource allocation and project prioritization.

9. **Empower Project Leaders**: Empower project leaders with the authority to make decisions and manage resources effectively. Provide training and support to enhance their project management skills.

10. **Encourage Continuous Improvement**: Promote a culture of continuous improvement by encouraging teams to

identify opportunities for enhancing processes and resource utilization. This culture fosters innovation and efficiency across all projects.

Balancing resources and priorities is essential for the successful management of multiple Six Sigma projects. By implementing strategic planning, resource allocation, and project management practices, organizations can optimize their use of resources, align projects with business goals, and achieve desired outcomes. This approach ensures that Six Sigma initiatives deliver maximum value and contribute to the organization's long-term success and competitiveness.

Chapter 7: Overcoming Challenges in Implementation

Common Obstacles and Pitfalls: Challenges organizations face when implementing DMAIC and DMADV.

Overcoming Challenges in Implementation

Implementing DMAIC and DMADV methodologies in Six Sigma presents a unique set of challenges and obstacles. Organizations often encounter these hurdles due to various factors, including resistance to change, inadequate training, and misalignment with organizational goals. Understanding these challenges is the first step toward effectively addressing them.

One of the most significant challenges is resistance to change. Employees may be reluctant to adopt new methodologies due to a lack of understanding or fear of the unknown. This resistance can be rooted in the perception that these new processes will add complexity or increase workload without clear benefits. It is crucial for organizations to communicate the value of Six Sigma clearly, emphasizing how it can streamline processes and lead to measurable improvements.

Another common obstacle is inadequate training and resources. Successful implementation of DMAIC and DMADV requires a deep understanding of the methodologies and the tools associated with each phase. Organizations often underestimate the investment needed in training and development, leading to poorly equipped teams that struggle to apply the concepts effectively. Providing comprehensive training and ongoing support is essential to empower employees to utilize Six Sigma tools confidently.

Misalignment with organizational goals is also a frequent pitfall. When Six Sigma initiatives are not aligned with the strategic objectives of the organization, they can lead to projects that do not deliver the desired impact. This misalignment can result in wasted resources and frustration among team members. Ensuring that Six Sigma projects are carefully selected and aligned with the organization's strategic priorities is crucial for maximizing their effectiveness.

Furthermore, inadequate data management can hinder the success of DMAIC and DMADV projects. These methodologies rely heavily on data analysis to drive decision-making and improvements. Poor data quality, lack of data availability, or ineffective data collection processes can lead to inaccurate conclusions and ineffective solutions. Implementing robust data management practices and investing in the right tools can significantly enhance the quality and reliability of data used in Six Sigma projects.

Lastly, sustaining the momentum and benefits of Six Sigma initiatives can be challenging. Organizations may experience initial success but struggle to maintain improvements over the long term. This issue often arises from a lack of a continuous improvement culture and insufficient mechanisms to monitor and sustain changes. Developing a culture that values continuous improvement and establishing processes to regularly review and adjust initiatives are vital for maintaining the gains achieved through Six Sigma.

By recognizing these common obstacles and pitfalls, organizations can better prepare for successful implementation of DMAIC and DMADV methodologies. Addressing these challenges requires a strategic approach, clear communication, and a commitment to continuous learning and improvement.

Strategies for Success: Tips and best practices for overcoming these challenges.

Strategies for Success

Overcoming the challenges associated with implementing DMAIC and DMADV methodologies requires a strategic and proactive approach. By adopting effective strategies and best practices, organizations can enhance their ability to implement Six Sigma successfully and achieve lasting improvements.

One of the most critical strategies for overcoming resistance to change is effective communication. It is essential to clearly articulate the benefits of Six Sigma and how it aligns with the organization's overall goals. This can be achieved by sharing success stories, demonstrating measurable results, and involving employees in the decision-making process. Engaging employees early on and seeking their input fosters a sense of ownership and commitment to the new methodologies.

Comprehensive training programs are another cornerstone of success. Investing in thorough and ongoing training ensures that employees have the necessary skills and knowledge to apply DMAIC and DMADV effectively. Training should be tailored to the specific needs of different roles within the organization and include hands-on workshops, case studies, and real-world examples. Providing access to experienced mentors and coaches can further support employees in their learning journey.

To address the challenge of misalignment with organizational goals, it is crucial to establish a clear link between Six Sigma initiatives and strategic priorities. This involves selecting projects that directly contribute to the organization's objectives and setting measurable goals and targets. Regularly reviewing the alignment of Six Sigma projects with business goals ensures that resources are focused on initiatives that deliver the most significant impact.

Effective data management is essential for the success of DMAIC and DMADV projects. Organizations should invest in robust data collection and analysis tools to ensure data accuracy and reliability. Establishing standardized data collection processes and providing training on data analysis techniques enhances the quality of insights derived from data. Additionally, fostering a data-driven culture encourages employees to make decisions based on evidence and analytics rather than intuition or assumptions.

Sustaining the momentum and benefits of Six Sigma requires a focus on building a continuous improvement culture. Organizations can achieve this by celebrating successes, recognizing and rewarding contributions, and creating opportunities for ongoing learning and development. Regularly reviewing and refining processes and encouraging teams to identify new improvement opportunities help maintain the momentum and drive innovation.

Leadership plays a vital role in the success of Six Sigma initiatives. Leaders should model the behaviors and attitudes they wish to see in their teams, demonstrating commitment to Six Sigma principles and actively participating in improvement efforts. Providing clear direction, setting realistic expectations, and supporting teams in overcoming obstacles contribute to a positive environment that fosters success.

By implementing these strategies and best practices, organizations can effectively overcome the challenges associated with DMAIC and DMADV methodologies. A commitment to continuous improvement, effective communication, and alignment with organizational goals ensures that Six Sigma becomes an integral part of the organization's DNA, driving sustainable success and growth.

Leadership and Change Management: The role of leadership in supporting Six Sigma initiatives.

Leadership and Change Management

Leadership plays a pivotal role in the successful implementation and sustainability of Six Sigma initiatives. The support and involvement of leaders are crucial in fostering a culture of continuous improvement and ensuring that DMAIC and DMADV methodologies are effectively integrated into the organization's operations.

A key responsibility of leadership is to provide a clear vision and direction for Six Sigma initiatives. Leaders must articulate the strategic importance of Six Sigma and how it aligns with the organization's overall goals. By communicating a compelling vision, leaders inspire employees to embrace change and commit to achieving the desired outcomes. This vision should be reinforced through regular communication and engagement with all levels of the organization.

Effective change management is essential for overcoming resistance and facilitating the adoption of Six Sigma methodologies. Leaders must actively manage the change process, addressing concerns and barriers that may arise. This involves listening to employees, understanding their perspectives, and providing the necessary support to ease the transition. By involving employees in the change process and encouraging their participation, leaders can foster a sense of ownership and commitment to the new methodologies.

Leadership also plays a critical role in providing resources and support for Six Sigma initiatives. This includes allocating sufficient resources for training, tools, and technology to enable teams to implement DMAIC and DMADV effectively. Leaders should prioritize investing in employee development, ensuring that teams have the skills and knowledge required to succeed. Additionally, leaders must empower employees by granting them the autonomy and authority to make decisions and take action in line with Six Sigma principles.

Creating a culture of accountability and recognition is another important aspect of leadership in Six Sigma. Leaders should set clear expectations and hold teams accountable for their performance. Regularly reviewing progress and providing feedback helps ensure that teams stay on track and make necessary adjustments. Recognizing and celebrating successes, whether big or small, reinforces positive behaviors and motivates teams to continue striving for excellence.

Moreover, leaders should model the behaviors they wish to see in their teams. Demonstrating a commitment to Six Sigma principles and actively participating in improvement efforts sends a strong message that quality and continuous improvement are valued at all levels of the organization. By leading by example, leaders inspire their teams to adopt the same mindset and approach.

In summary, leadership and change management are critical to the success of Six Sigma initiatives. By providing a clear vision, managing change effectively, allocating resources, fostering accountability, and leading by example, leaders create an environment where DMAIC and DMADV methodologies can thrive. Through their support and involvement, leaders drive the successful implementation and sustainability of Six Sigma, leading to improved processes, enhanced performance, and long-term success.

Chapter 8:
Measuring and Sustaining Success

Key Performance Indicators

Key performance indicators (KPIs) are essential tools for measuring the success of Six Sigma projects. They provide quantifiable metrics that help organizations evaluate the effectiveness of their DMAIC and DMADV initiatives and ensure that they achieve their desired outcomes. Selecting the right KPIs is critical for accurately assessing performance and driving continuous improvement.

One of the most common KPIs in Six Sigma is the defect rate. This metric measures the number of defects or errors in a process relative to the total number of opportunities for error. A lower defect rate indicates higher quality and process efficiency. Organizations often use the Six Sigma metric of defects per million opportunities (DPMO) to benchmark performance against industry standards and track improvements over time.

Cycle time is another important KPI for Six Sigma projects. It measures the time it takes to complete a process from start to finish. Reducing cycle time can lead to increased efficiency, faster delivery of products or services, and improved customer satisfaction. Monitoring cycle time helps organizations identify bottlenecks and inefficiencies that can be addressed through DMAIC and DMADV methodologies.

Cost savings is a critical KPI that quantifies the financial impact of Six Sigma projects. By identifying and eliminating waste, improving processes, and reducing defects, organizations can achieve significant cost reductions. Measuring cost savings helps demonstrate the value of

Six Sigma initiatives to stakeholders and reinforces the importance of continuous improvement efforts.

Customer satisfaction is another key metric for evaluating the success of Six Sigma projects. Organizations can use surveys, feedback forms, and other tools to gather customer insights and assess their satisfaction with products or services. Improvements in customer satisfaction indicate that Six Sigma initiatives are effectively addressing customer needs and enhancing the overall experience.

Process capability is a KPI that measures the ability of a process to produce outputs within specified limits. It is often expressed as a process capability index (Cpk) or process performance index (Ppk). A higher process capability indicates that a process is stable and capable of consistently delivering high-quality results. Monitoring process capability helps organizations identify areas for improvement and ensure that processes remain within acceptable limits.

Employee engagement and participation in Six Sigma projects are also important indicators of success. High levels of engagement and participation suggest that employees are committed to the initiatives and actively contributing to process improvements. Organizations can measure engagement through surveys, feedback, and participation rates in Six Sigma activities.

In conclusion, selecting and monitoring the right KPIs is crucial for measuring the success of Six Sigma projects. Defect rates, cycle time, cost savings, customer satisfaction, process capability, and employee engagement are among the key metrics that provide valuable insights into the effectiveness of DMAIC and DMADV initiatives. By regularly evaluating these KPIs, organizations can ensure that their Six Sigma efforts lead to sustainable improvements and achieve their strategic objectives.

Sustaining Improvements

Sustaining the improvements achieved through Six Sigma initiatives is crucial for ensuring long-term success and fostering a culture of continuous improvement. While achieving initial success is important, maintaining and building upon these gains requires a strategic approach and a commitment to ongoing development.

One of the most effective strategies for sustaining improvements is embedding a culture of continuous improvement within the organization. This involves promoting a mindset where employees are encouraged to identify opportunities for enhancement and innovation in their daily work. Leaders play a pivotal role in nurturing this culture by modeling continuous improvement behaviors and recognizing and rewarding contributions that drive positive change.

Standardizing processes is another critical strategy for maintaining improvements. Once improvements are identified and implemented, it is essential to document the new processes and establish standard operating procedures (SOPs) that ensure consistency and repeatability. Standardization helps prevent deviations and ensures that improvements are sustained over time. Regularly reviewing and updating SOPs based on feedback and changing needs helps maintain their relevance and effectiveness.

Continuous monitoring and evaluation are essential for sustaining improvements. Organizations should establish mechanisms to track key performance indicators (KPIs) and monitor process performance regularly. This allows for the early detection of deviations or issues that may impact the sustainability of improvements. By addressing these challenges promptly, organizations can prevent regression and maintain the gains achieved through Six Sigma initiatives.

Engaging employees in ongoing improvement efforts is crucial for sustaining success. Organizations should provide opportunities for employees to participate in improvement projects, share their ideas, and contribute to problem-solving initiatives. Encouraging cross-functional collaboration and knowledge sharing helps build a sense of ownership and commitment to continuous improvement across the organization.

Investing in ongoing training and development is also vital for sustaining improvements. Providing employees with opportunities to enhance their skills and knowledge ensures that they are equipped to drive improvement efforts effectively. Training programs should be tailored to meet the evolving needs of the organization and include topics such as advanced Six Sigma techniques, data analysis, and change management.

Celebrating successes and recognizing achievements is an important strategy for maintaining momentum. Acknowledging the contributions of individuals and teams reinforces positive behaviors and motivates others to participate in improvement efforts. Celebrations and recognition events provide an opportunity to reflect on achievements, share success stories, and inspire further progress.

Finally, integrating Six Sigma principles into the organization's strategic planning and decision-making processes is key to sustaining improvements. By aligning Six Sigma initiatives with the organization's goals and objectives, organizations can ensure that continuous improvement remains a priority and receives the necessary support and resources.

In summary, sustaining improvements achieved through Six Sigma requires a strategic and holistic approach. By fostering a culture of continuous improvement, standardizing processes, engaging employees, investing in training, and integrating Six Sigma into strategic planning, organizations can maintain the gains achieved and drive ongoing progress. These strategies ensure that Six Sigma becomes an integral part of the organization's DNA, leading to sustained success and growth.

Case Study: XYZ Manufacturing

Background

XYZ Manufacturing, a leading producer of automotive components, faced challenges with product quality and production efficiency. The company experienced frequent defects and delays, impacting customer satisfaction and profitability. To address these issues, XYZ Manufacturing decided to implement Six Sigma methodologies, focusing on both DMAIC and DMADV approaches to drive improvements and innovation.

Implementation of DMAIC

The company started by applying the DMAIC methodology to its existing production processes. The team identified the most critical processes affecting quality and efficiency and defined specific goals for improvement. They used data-driven analysis to measure current performance, revealing significant variations and bottlenecks in production.

During the Analyze phase, XYZ Manufacturing identified the root causes of defects and inefficiencies. These included outdated equipment, inconsistent quality control procedures, and insufficient employee training. The company implemented targeted improvements, such as upgrading machinery, standardizing quality checks, and providing comprehensive training programs.

In the Improve phase, XYZ Manufacturing introduced process changes to address identified issues. They implemented real-time monitoring systems to track production metrics and quickly address deviations. Additionally, they optimized workflows to eliminate unnecessary steps and reduce cycle time. These improvements led to a 30% reduction in defects and a 20% increase in production efficiency.

The Control phase focused on sustaining these improvements. The company established robust monitoring and feedback mechanisms to ensure ongoing adherence to new procedures. Regular audits and reviews helped maintain process stability and prevent regression. As a result, the company achieved sustained improvements in product quality and operational efficiency.

Implementation of DMADV

XYZ Manufacturing also applied the DMADV methodology to develop a new product line. The company aimed to create a high-performance component that met evolving customer demands and industry standards. They began by defining customer requirements and design specifications.

The Measure and Analyze phases involved extensive research and prototyping to explore various design options. The team used advanced simulation tools to evaluate different configurations and materials. This data-driven approach allowed them to identify the most promising design that met performance, cost, and sustainability criteria.

In the Design phase, XYZ Manufacturing developed detailed plans for the new component. They collaborated closely with suppliers to ensure the availability of high-quality materials and components. Rigorous testing and validation processes were conducted to verify the design's performance and reliability.

The Verify phase involved pilot production and market testing. XYZ Manufacturing collected customer feedback and made final adjustments to the design and manufacturing processes. The successful launch of the new product line resulted in increased market share and customer satisfaction.

Sustaining Success

XYZ Manufacturing's commitment to sustaining improvements was evident in its continuous improvement culture. The company integrated Six Sigma principles into its strategic planning, ensuring that improvement initiatives aligned with long-term goals. Regular training sessions and knowledge-sharing events reinforced a culture of learning and innovation.

Leadership played a crucial role in sustaining success. The company's leaders actively participated in improvement efforts, providing support and resources to drive progress. They celebrated achievements and recognized employee contributions, fostering a sense of ownership and pride in the organization's accomplishments.

By leveraging DMAIC and DMADV methodologies, XYZ Manufacturing achieved significant improvements in product quality, operational efficiency, and innovation. The company's success demonstrates the power of Six Sigma in driving sustainable change and delivering value to customers and stakeholders.

Chapter 9:
The Future of Six Sigma

Emerging Trends and Innovations

As the business landscape continues to evolve, so does the application of Six Sigma methodologies. With the rapid advancement of technology and the growing demand for innovation, Six Sigma is adapting to meet the needs of modern organizations. Emerging trends and innovations are shaping the future of Six Sigma, making it more versatile and impactful than ever before.

One of the most significant trends in Six Sigma is the integration of digital technologies. The rise of big data and analytics has transformed the way organizations approach process improvement. By leveraging advanced data analysis tools and techniques, Six Sigma practitioners can gain deeper insights into process performance and identify improvement opportunities more accurately and efficiently. Predictive analytics and machine learning algorithms enable organizations to anticipate issues before they arise and optimize processes in real time.

The Internet of Things (IoT) is another technological advancement driving the evolution of Six Sigma. IoT devices collect vast amounts of data from various sources, providing real-time insights into process conditions and performance. This data allows organizations to monitor processes continuously, identify deviations, and implement corrective actions promptly. IoT-enabled Six Sigma initiatives enhance operational efficiency, reduce downtime, and improve overall quality.

Agile methodologies are also influencing the future of Six Sigma. The principles of agility, such as flexibility, collaboration, and iterative improvement, align well with Six Sigma's focus on continuous enhancement. Organizations are increasingly integrating Agile and Six Sigma approaches, known as Agile Six Sigma, to create more adaptable and responsive improvement processes. This integration allows teams to quickly address changing customer needs and market conditions while maintaining a structured approach to quality improvement.

The rise of remote work and virtual collaboration tools has also impacted Six Sigma practices. With teams distributed across different locations, organizations are leveraging digital platforms to facilitate collaboration and communication. Virtual Six Sigma projects enable cross-functional teams to work together seamlessly, regardless of geographic boundaries. These tools enhance the ability to share knowledge, track progress, and manage projects efficiently, ensuring that Six Sigma initiatives remain effective in a digital-first world.

Sustainability and social responsibility are becoming increasingly important considerations for organizations. Six Sigma is evolving to incorporate these values into improvement efforts. Sustainable Six Sigma focuses on reducing waste, optimizing resource usage, and minimizing environmental impact while maintaining quality and efficiency. By integrating sustainability goals into Six Sigma projects, organizations can align their improvement efforts with broader environmental and social objectives.

Finally, the future of Six Sigma is being shaped by the growing emphasis on customer experience. Organizations are recognizing the importance of delivering exceptional customer value and satisfaction. Six Sigma methodologies are being applied to enhance customer experiences by identifying and addressing pain points, streamlining processes, and ensuring consistent quality. By placing the customer at the center of improvement efforts, organizations can build stronger relationships and drive long-term loyalty.

In summary, the future of Six Sigma is being shaped by emerging trends and innovations that enhance its effectiveness and relevance. Digital technologies, Agile methodologies, remote collaboration, sustainability, and customer-centric approaches are driving the evolution of Six Sigma practices. By embracing these trends, organizations can continue to leverage Six Sigma to achieve sustainable success and meet the demands of an ever-changing business environment.

The Role of Six Sigma in Modern Business

In today's rapidly changing business environment, organizations face increasing pressure to remain competitive and deliver exceptional value to customers. Six Sigma, with its focus on quality improvement and process optimization, continues to play a crucial role in helping organizations meet these challenges. By leveraging Six Sigma methodologies, businesses can achieve operational excellence, enhance customer satisfaction, and drive sustainable growth.

One of the primary ways Six Sigma helps organizations remain competitive is by improving process efficiency. Six Sigma methodologies, such as DMAIC and DMADV, provide a structured approach to identifying and eliminating waste, reducing variability, and optimizing workflows. By streamlining processes, organizations can reduce costs, increase productivity, and deliver products and services more quickly and reliably. These improvements enhance operational efficiency and contribute to a stronger competitive position in the market.

Quality is a critical differentiator in today's competitive landscape. Six Sigma's emphasis on reducing defects and improving quality helps organizations deliver products and services that meet or exceed customer expectations. By consistently producing high-quality offerings, businesses can build strong customer loyalty and reputation. This focus on quality not only attracts new customers but also retains existing ones, driving long-term success.

In addition to improving quality and efficiency, Six Sigma enables organizations to make data-driven decisions. The methodologies involve rigorous data collection and analysis, providing valuable insights into process performance and customer behavior. By leveraging data, organizations can identify trends, anticipate customer needs, and make informed strategic decisions. This analytical approach allows businesses to respond quickly to market changes and stay ahead of the competition.

Six Sigma also plays a vital role in fostering a culture of continuous improvement within organizations. By promoting a mindset of ongoing enhancement, Six Sigma encourages employees to identify and address inefficiencies, explore innovative solutions, and drive positive change. This culture of continuous improvement empowers organizations to adapt to evolving market conditions and capitalize on new opportunities, ensuring sustained competitiveness.

Furthermore, Six Sigma helps organizations align their improvement efforts with strategic objectives. By focusing on projects that directly contribute to the organization's goals, businesses can ensure that their resources are directed toward initiatives that deliver the most significant impact. This alignment between Six Sigma initiatives and strategic priorities enhances the organization's ability to achieve its mission and vision.

Incorporating Six Sigma into modern business practices also supports organizations in addressing sustainability and social responsibility. By reducing waste, optimizing resource usage, and minimizing environmental impact, Six Sigma initiatives contribute to more sustainable operations. This commitment to sustainability not only meets regulatory requirements but also aligns with the growing demand for environmentally and socially responsible business practices.

In summary, Six Sigma continues to be a vital tool for organizations seeking to remain competitive in the modern business landscape. By improving process efficiency, enhancing quality, enabling data-driven decision-making, fostering continuous improvement, and aligning with strategic objectives, Six Sigma empowers organizations to achieve operational excellence and drive sustainable growth. As businesses navigate an ever-changing environment, Six Sigma remains a powerful methodology for achieving long-term success.

Conclusion

Recap of Key Points

Throughout this book, we have explored the transformative power of Six Sigma methodologies and their impact on organizations striving for excellence in a competitive business environment. By delving into the intricacies of DMAIC and DMADV, we have uncovered the strategic approaches that drive quality improvement, process optimization, and innovation.

We began with an understanding of the foundational principles of Six Sigma, highlighting its origins and evolution. Six Sigma emerged as a robust methodology for reducing defects, improving quality, and enhancing efficiency. Its systematic approach, grounded in data-driven decision-making, has made it an indispensable tool for organizations across industries.

In exploring the DMAIC framework, we examined each of its five phases—Define, Measure, Analyze, Improve, and Control. This methodology provides a structured process for identifying and addressing inefficiencies, optimizing workflows, and achieving sustainable improvements. Through real-world examples, we saw how DMAIC empowers organizations to deliver high-quality products and services while reducing costs and enhancing customer satisfaction.

We also delved into the DMADV methodology, emphasizing its role in designing and developing new processes and products. The five phases of DMADV—Define, Measure, Analyze, Design, and Verify—enable organizations to innovate and create solutions that meet customer needs and exceed expectations. By integrating DMADV into their innovation strategies, businesses can stay ahead of the competition and drive market success.

Our exploration of Six Sigma's tools and techniques showcased the versatility and adaptability of this methodology. From data collection and analysis to problem-solving techniques, Six Sigma equips organizations with the means to make informed decisions and implement effective improvements. These tools are integral to achieving process excellence and fostering a culture of continuous improvement.

We highlighted the importance of integrating Six Sigma into business strategy, emphasizing its alignment with organizational goals and objectives. By selecting projects that directly contribute to strategic priorities, organizations can maximize the impact of their Six Sigma initiatives and ensure long-term success.

Addressing the challenges of implementation, we explored strategies for overcoming obstacles and pitfalls, underscoring the role of leadership and change management. Leadership support and effective communication are critical in fostering a culture that embraces Six Sigma principles and drives continuous improvement.

As we looked to the future, we identified emerging trends and innovations shaping the evolution of Six Sigma. The integration of digital technologies, Agile methodologies, and sustainability considerations is enhancing the effectiveness and relevance of Six Sigma in modern business.

In summary, Six Sigma is a powerful methodology that empowers organizations to achieve operational excellence, enhance customer satisfaction, and drive sustainable growth. By embracing Six Sigma principles and methodologies, businesses can navigate an ever-changing environment, remain competitive, and achieve their strategic objectives.

Call to Action

As we conclude our exploration of Six Sigma, it is time to take the insights and strategies shared in this book and put them into action. The journey toward operational excellence and continuous improvement begins with a commitment to embrace Six Sigma methodologies—DMAIC and DMADV—in your organization.

Six Sigma offers a powerful framework for driving quality improvement, process optimization, and innovation. By adopting DMAIC, you can systematically identify and eliminate inefficiencies, reduce defects, and enhance customer satisfaction. The structured approach of DMAIC empowers your team to analyze processes, implement improvements, and sustain long-term success. Similarly, DMADV equips your organization with the tools to design and develop innovative products and services that meet and exceed customer expectations.

The path to success with Six Sigma starts with a decision to prioritize quality and continuous improvement. It requires a commitment from leadership to support and champion Six Sigma initiatives. As a leader, you have the power to inspire your team, communicate the vision, and create an environment that values excellence and innovation.

Begin by identifying key processes or areas in your organization that can benefit from Six Sigma methodologies. Engage your team in the process, encouraging collaboration and open communication. Provide the necessary training and resources to equip your employees with the skills and knowledge to drive Six Sigma projects effectively.

Remember that Six Sigma is not just a one-time initiative but a journey toward ongoing improvement. Foster a culture that embraces change, encourages experimentation, and celebrates successes. Continuously monitor and evaluate your progress, using key performance indicators to measure the impact of your efforts. Share your achievements with your organization, reinforcing the value of Six Sigma in achieving strategic goals.

By applying DMAIC and DMADV, you can unlock the full potential of your organization. You can deliver exceptional value to your customers, increase operational efficiency, and remain competitive in a rapidly changing business landscape. The benefits of Six Sigma extend beyond improved processes; they lead to a stronger, more resilient organization poised for future success.

Take the first step today. Embrace the principles of Six Sigma and embark on a journey of transformation and excellence. The future of your organization depends on your willingness to innovate, improve, and lead with purpose. Together, let us create a brighter future, one process at a time.

Appendices

Glossary of Terms

6S (Six Sigma) Methodology: A set of techniques and tools for process improvement aimed at reducing defects and variability in manufacturing and business processes.

Benchmarking: The process of comparing one's business processes and performance metrics to industry bests or best practices from other companies.

Cause-and-Effect Diagram (Fishbone Diagram): A visual tool used to identify, explore, and display the possible causes of a particular problem, helping teams identify root causes.

Control Chart: A statistical tool used to monitor the stability of a process over time by plotting data points and identifying trends or variations.

Control Phase: The final phase of DMAIC, where improvements are maintained through monitoring and control plans to ensure consistent performance.

Critical to Quality (CTQ): Key measurable characteristics of a product or process that must meet performance standards to satisfy customer needs.

Defect: Any instance where a product or process fails to meet customer specifications or expectations.

Defects Per Million Opportunities (DPMO): A metric used to measure the number of defects in a process per one million opportunities for a defect to occur.

Design for Six Sigma (DFSS): An approach to designing products and processes that meet Six Sigma standards from the outset, focusing on quality and reliability.

DMAIC: An acronym for Define, Measure, Analyze, Improve, and Control, representing the five phases of a Six Sigma process improvement project.

DMADV: An acronym for Define, Measure, Analyze, Design, and Verify, representing the five phases of a Six Sigma process design project.

Failure Mode and Effects Analysis (FMEA): A systematic method for evaluating processes to identify potential failures and their effects, prioritizing actions to mitigate risk.

Gemba: A Japanese term meaning "the real place," used in Six Sigma to refer to the location where work is performed and value is created.

Histogram: A graphical representation of data distribution, used to visualize the frequency of data points within specified ranges.

Kaizen: A Japanese philosophy of continuous improvement, focusing on small, incremental changes that lead to significant improvements over time.

Lean Six Sigma: A methodology that combines the principles of Lean (waste reduction) and Six Sigma (variation reduction) to improve process efficiency and quality.

Pareto Chart: A bar graph that represents the frequency or impact of problems, helping teams identify the most significant issues to address.

Process Capability Index (Cpk): A statistical measure of a process's ability to produce outputs within specified limits, indicating how well a process meets specifications.

Root Cause Analysis: A method of problem-solving that identifies the underlying causes of defects or issues, allowing for targeted improvements.

SIPOC Diagram: A tool used to identify the Suppliers, Inputs, Process, Outputs, and Customers of a process, providing a high-level view of process components.

Statistical Process Control (SPC): A method of monitoring and controlling processes using statistical techniques to ensure process stability and quality.

Value Stream Mapping: A visual tool used to analyze and improve the flow of materials and information required to deliver a product or service to customers.

Voice of the Customer (VOC): A process used to capture customer requirements and feedback, ensuring that products and services meet their needs and expectations.

Further Reading and Resources

Books

1. **"The Lean Six Sigma Pocket Toolbook" by Michael L. George, John Maxey, David Rowlands, and Mark Price:** A comprehensive guide that provides an overview of Lean Six Sigma concepts and tools, offering practical insights for applying these methodologies in various industries.

2. **"Lean Six Sigma for Dummies" by John Morgan and Martin Brenig-Jones:** A beginner-friendly introduction to Lean Six Sigma, covering the basics of the methodology and providing practical tips for implementation.

3. **"The Six Sigma Handbook" by Thomas Pyzdek and Paul Keller:** A detailed reference book covering Six Sigma principles, tools, and techniques, offering in-depth knowledge for practitioners and leaders.

4. **"The Goal: A Process of Ongoing Improvement" by Eliyahu M. Goldratt and Jeff Cox:** A business novel that explores the theory of constraints and process improvement, providing valuable insights into the application of Lean and Six Sigma principles.

5. **"Toyota Production System: Beyond Large-Scale Production" by Taiichi Ohno:** A foundational text on Lean manufacturing and the Toyota Production System, offering insights into the principles that have influenced Six Sigma practices.

Articles

1. **"What is Six Sigma?" by Peter Pande and Larry Holpp (Harvard Business Review):** An article that provides an overview of Six Sigma methodologies and their impact on business performance.

2. **"Six Sigma: A Retrospective and Prospective Study" by Rahul Jain and Rajesh K. Tyagi (Quality Management Journal):** A research article that examines the evolution and future directions of Six Sigma methodologies.

3. **"The Role of Leadership in Six Sigma Implementation: A Review" by Peter K. Moran and Anil Khurana (Journal of Quality & Reliability Engineering):** An article exploring the critical role of leadership in successfully implementing Six Sigma initiatives.

Websites

1. **American Society for Quality (ASQ) - Six Sigma Resource Center:** A comprehensive online resource offering articles, case studies, and tools related to Six Sigma and quality management. ASQ Six Sigma Resource Center

2. **Six Sigma Daily:** An online publication that provides news, insights, and practical tips on Six Sigma and Lean methodologies. Six Sigma Daily

3. **Lean Six Sigma Institute:** A resource hub for Lean Six Sigma training, certifications, and resources. Lean Six Sigma Institute

4. **Process Excellence Network (PEX Network):** An online community and resource center for process improvement professionals, offering articles, webinars, and case studies. PEX Network

5. **iSixSigma:** A popular website offering a wealth of information, articles, and forums on Six Sigma, Lean, and process improvement. iSixSigma

DMAIC Templates and Tools

1. Project Charter Template

A Project Charter is a foundational document that outlines the scope, objectives, and stakeholders of a Six Sigma project.

- ➢ **Project Title**
- ➢ **Project Leader and Team Members**
- ➢ **Business Case**
- ➢ **Problem Statement**
- ➢ **Goal Statement**
- ➢ **Scope**
- ➢ **Timeline**
- ➢ **Key Stakeholders**
- ➢ **Resources Required**

2. SIPOC Diagram

A SIPOC (Suppliers, Inputs, Process, Outputs, Customers) diagram provides a high-level view of a process, helping teams identify key components and stakeholders.

- ➤ **Suppliers:** Who provides the inputs?
- ➤ **Inputs:** What materials, information, or resources are needed?
- ➤ **Process:** What are the major steps in the process?
- ➤ **Outputs:** What are the final products or services?
- ➤ **Customers:** Who receives the outputs?

3. Cause-and-Effect Diagram (Fishbone Diagram)

This tool helps identify potential causes of a problem, allowing teams to explore root causes.

- ➤ **Categories:** Typical categories include Methods, Materials, Equipment, People, Environment, and Measurements.
- ➤ **Potential Causes:** List specific causes under each category.

4. Control Plan Template

A Control Plan outlines the monitoring and control measures needed to sustain improvements.

- ➤ **Process Step**
- ➤ **Potential Failure Mode**
- ➤ **Control Measure**
- ➤ **Responsibility**
- ➤ **Frequency of Monitoring**

DMADV Templates and Tools

1. Quality Function Deployment (QFD) Matrix

A QFD Matrix helps translate customer requirements into technical specifications.

- ➤ **Customer Requirements (Whats)**

- Technical Requirements (Hows)
- Relationships Matrix
- Prioritization and Weighting

2. Design of Experiments (DOE) Template

DOE is a structured method for determining the relationship between factors affecting a process and the output of that process.

- Objective
- Factors and Levels
- Response Variables
- Experimental Design
- Results and Analysis

3. Failure Mode and Effects Analysis (FMEA) Template

FMEA identifies potential failure modes and their impact on process performance.

- Process Step
- Potential Failure Mode
- Effects of Failure
- Severity Rating
- Potential Causes
- Occurrence Rating
- Detection Controls
- Detection Rating
- Risk Priority Number (RPN)
- Recommended Actions

4. Verification Plan Template

A Verification Plan outlines the steps to confirm that the design meets the specified requirements.

- Requirement
- Verification Method (e.g., Testing, Inspection)
- Acceptance Criteria

- ➤ **Responsible Person**
- ➤ **Timeline**

Tools for Both DMAIC and DMADV

1. Control Charts

Used to monitor process stability and performance over time, control charts help identify variations and trends.

- ➤ **Data Collection Frequency**
- ➤ **Upper and Lower Control Limits**
- ➤ **Process Mean**

2. Pareto Analysis

A Pareto Chart identifies the most significant factors contributing to a problem, based on the Pareto Principle (80/20 rule).

- ➤ **Categories of Issues**
- ➤ **Frequency or Impact of Each Issue**
- ➤ **Cumulative Percentage**

3. Root Cause Analysis

Tools such as 5 Whys and Cause-and-Effect Diagrams aid in identifying the underlying causes of a problem.

- ➤ **Problem Statement**
- ➤ **5 Whys Analysis**
- ➤ **Fishbone Diagram**

www.ingramcontent.com/pod-product-compliance
Lightning Source LLC
Chambersburg PA
CBHW050329230526
45471CB00005B/2408